ACTUAL
HR-Approved Ways
To Tell Coworkers
They're Stupid

75 Witty Alternatives for Those Things
You Want to Say At Work But Can't

SWEET HARMONY PRESS

This book is for entertainment purposes only. No certified HR professional was involved in the creation of this humor book. Use it at your own discretion.

Print ISBN: 978-1-948713-46-7

For inquiries for bulk or wholesale orders, contact info@sweetharmonypress.com

Instead of getting fired by saying:

> **"WTF are you even talking about?"**

Maybe try:

> *"I'm not sure I fully grasp your perspective. Can you explain it further?"*

Instead of getting fired by saying:

> **"That is literally the dumbest idea I have ever heard"**

Maybe try:

> *"I value your input, but I have some concerns."*

Instead of getting fired by saying:

"That is utter bullsh*t"

Maybe try:

"I'm not entirely convinced by that argument."

Instead of getting fired by saying:

"You're wrong, but I'll let you figure it out yourself."

Maybe try:

"Let me know if you get stuck on that or would like some fresh ideas."

Instead of getting fired by saying:

"I love it when you take credit for my ideas."

Maybe try:

"I'm glad you agree with my ideas. Can I help you present them to the directors?"

Instead of getting fired by saying:

> **"Did you even read my f*cking email?"**

Maybe try:

> *"Let me restate what I said in my email."*

Instead of getting fired by saying:

> **"You have been here two minutes and want to change everything. How 'bout paying attention for a while first, dumbass?"**

Maybe try:

> *"I would be happy to review our procedures with you and why they are in place."*

Instead of getting fired by saying:

"Your idea is terrible, but I'll pretend to consider it."

Maybe try:

"Can we discuss the pros and cons of this approach?"

Instead of getting fired by saying:

"Do you even have any idea what you are doing?"

Maybe try:

"Can we review this together to ensure we're on the same page?"

Instead of getting fired by saying:

> **"No, we don't need any more effing slides."**

Maybe try:

> *"I think all the information is covered already."*

Instead of getting fired by saying:

> **"And just how the f*ck do you expect me to do that?"**

Maybe try:

> *"Can you tell me how you would approach achieving that?"*

Instead of getting fired by saying:

"This place is complete chaos"

Maybe try:

"Perhaps we should discuss an initiative for some process improvements?"

Instead of getting fired by saying:

> **"I can't believe they pay you for this."**

Maybe try:

> *"Maybe you should check if there are other tasks you can help with."*

Instead of getting fired by saying:

> "Eww, creep, no I don't want to "get to know each other better" over a drink.

Maybe try:

> No.

Instead of getting fired by saying:

"Your incompetence is truly astonishing."

Maybe try:

"I think there are better ways to accomplish this."

Instead of getting fired by saying:

"**Please stop micromanaging me.**"

Maybe try:

"*I will let you know if I need more guidance, but I have it from here.*"

Instead of getting fired by saying:

"You talk way too much for someone who says so little."

Maybe try:

"Let's focus on the task at hand."

Instead of getting fired by saying:

"I wish I could take as many breaks as you do."

Maybe try:

"How long will you be gone? I could use some help with this."

Instead of getting fired by saying:

"If you spent half as much time working as you do complaining, you'd get a lot more done."

Maybe try:

"Can you try working through the tough parts without complaining? Things might get done more quickly."

Instead of getting fired by saying:

> **"This is going to be a train wreck"**

Maybe try:

> *"Can we take a step back and reevaluate our options?"*

Instead of getting fired by saying:

"**Sure, I love doing your work too.**"

Maybe try:

"I can give you a hand with this today to meet the deadline, but let's figure out how to plan ahead better for next time."

Instead of getting fired by saying:

"I can't believe how
clueless you are
about what actually
happens here."

Maybe try:

"Can I have a meeting
with you to discuss some
of my concerns?"

Instead of getting fired by saying:

"Have you actually lost your f*cking mind?"

Maybe try:

"Can you tell me your line of reasoning about that?"

Instead of getting fired by saying:

> **"Sorry but I am not f*cking working nights and weekends to meet those unreasonable deadlines."**

Maybe try:

> *"We don't have the staff resources to meet that deadline. We will need to re-evaluate it."*

Instead of getting fired by saying:

"Can you just worry about your own damn work and stop telling me how to do my job?"

Maybe try:

"I've got this. Your constant input is distracting. I will let you know if I need help."

Instead of getting fired by saying:

> **"That may be the dumbest thing you have said this year"**

Maybe try:

> *"I appreciate your input, but I think we should reconsider."*

Instead of getting fired by saying:

> **"How are you not f*cking getting this?"**

Maybe try:

> *"I'm not sure how else to explain it. Which part confuses you?"*

Instead of getting fired by saying:

"**Your constant negativity is totally exhausting.**"

Maybe try:

"Negative remarks bring all of us down. Please try to be more constructive and positive."

Instead of getting fired by saying:

"**Your supreme lack of effort is really disappointing.**"

Maybe try:

"*We really need you to improve your output. Is there anything standing in the way of that?*"

Instead of getting fired by saying:

"No one cares about your personal problems, so please stop sharing."

Maybe try:

"For right now, we need to focus on the project goals. Let's try to keep our conversations work-related."

Instead of getting fired by saying:

"Your incompetence is screwing things up for the entire team."

Maybe try:

"We really need you to bring your best effort here. Are there parts of the assignment you don't understand?"

Instead of getting fired by saying:

"You always manage to take credit for other people's work."

Maybe try:

"Be sure to give credit to everyone who has contributed."

Instead of getting fired by saying:

"**Your political views are absolutely bat-shit crazy**"

Maybe try:

"Let's agree not to talk about politically-charged issues at work."

Instead of getting fired by saying:

"Your constant interruptions are hindering everyone's productivity."

Maybe try:

"If you need to discuss something, please keep a list and reserve a time on my calendar to discuss them all at once."

Instead of getting fired by saying:

"I doubt you'll ever understand the concept of punctuality."

Maybe try:

"It actually is important to be on-time for work and meetings."

Instead of getting fired by saying:

> **"Your lack of organization is causing complete chaos."**

Maybe try:

> *"Can we discuss implementing some better organizational methods?"*

Instead of getting fired by saying:

> **"Please stop using your authority to assert dominance, it's counterproductive."**

Maybe try:

> *"We are more productive when we work as equal teammates."*

Instead of getting fired by saying:

> **"You're so f*cking lazy, why don't you do any work?"**

Maybe try:

> *I noticed that you haven't finished your tasks yet. Is there something preventing this?*

Instead of getting fired by saying:

"Your ideas are terrible, and they never work."

Maybe try:

I appreciate your input, but have you considered an alternative approach?

Instead of getting fired by saying:

"Stop talking so loudly, it's annoying!"

Maybe try:

"I'm having trouble concentrating, do you mind lowering your volume a bit?"

Instead of getting fired by saying:

"Why do you always make everything about yourself?"

Maybe try:

I think it's important to consider other perspectives as well. Let's focus on the team's needs.

Instead of getting fired by saying:

"You're always so negative, lighten up!"

Maybe try:

Positivity is crucial in the workplace. How can we create a more uplifting environment?

Instead of getting fired by saying:

"I can't believe you made such a dumb mistake."

Maybe try:

I noticed an error in this report, let's work together to fix it.

Instead of getting fired by saying:

"You're way too slow, it's frustrating to work with you."

Maybe try:

"We have a tight deadline, can we find a more efficient way to complete this task?"

Instead of getting fired by saying:

"Am I speaking a different f*cking language?"

Maybe try:

"I think there might be a misunderstanding."

Instead of getting fired by saying:

"You have no manners, why don't you learn some?"

Maybe try:

Professionalism is important in our workplace. Let's focus on improving our communication skills.

Instead of getting fired by saying:

> **"Do you ever take your job seriously?"**

Maybe try:

> *I noticed some of the work hasn't been up to our usual standards. Is everything alright?"*

Instead of getting fired by saying:

"You're so clueless, you never understand what's going on."

Maybe try:

"It seems like there might be a communication gap, can we clarify expectations and roles?"

Instead of getting fired by saying:

"**Your total incompetence never fails to amaze me.**"

Maybe try:

"*Perhaps we can look into some training to help your performance.*"

Instead of getting fired by saying:

"You're lucky you have me to fix all your mistakes."

Maybe try:

"Maybe we can have a training session to avoid any errors in the future."

Instead of getting fired by saying:

"Your lack of attention to detail is astonishing."

Maybe try:

"Have you considered implementing a double-check system for accuracy?"

Instead of getting fired by saying:

"I see you're late again and expecting everyone to cover for you."

Maybe try:

"It's really important that you arrive on time. It makes a poor start to everyone's day."

Instead of getting fired by saying:

"You never contribute anything valuable in meetings."

Maybe try:

"During our next meeting can you bring one or two ideas for discussion?"

Instead of getting fired by saying:

"Did you completely forget how to do this task?"

Maybe try:

"If you need a refresher, I can walk you through the steps."

Instead of getting fired by saying:

"I'm glad I can always count on you to do nothing."

Maybe try:

"Let's review the expectations for your role?"

Instead of getting fired by saying:

"**Guess who messed up the report... again?**"

Maybe try:

"I think we need to review the report together to correct any mistakes."

Instead of getting fired by saying:

> **"Wow, your time management skills are impressive."**

Maybe try:

> *"Let's review your system for managing your tasks."*

Instead of getting fired by saying:

"You're like a black hole for productivity."

Maybe try:

"Do you have any suggestions to help increase your productivity?"

Instead of getting fired by saying:

"You've mastered the art of doing the bare minimum."

Maybe try:

"It seems you are quite comfortable in your role now. Let's find some new challenges for you."

Instead of getting fired by saying:

> **"Congratulations, you've aced another pointless task."**

Maybe try:

> *"I appreciate your attention to detail, even in smaller tasks. However, let's not forget the main objective."*

Instead of getting fired by saying:

"**Are you allergic to taking responsibility?**"

Maybe try:

"You need to accept responsibility when things go wrong."

Instead of getting fired by saying:

"Your ability to suck the energy out of the room is impressive."

Maybe try:

"We all work better when everyone is engaged."

Instead of getting fired by saying:

"I'm glad we can always rely on you to ruin the mood."

Maybe try:

"Is everything alright? You seem a bit down lately."

Instead of getting fired by saying:

"You have a true talent for spreading negativity."

Maybe try:

"Our culture requires maintaining a more positive atmosphere."

Instead of getting fired by saying:

"You should receive an award for most pointless comments."

Maybe try:

"Let's stay focused on the task at hand."

Instead of getting fired by saying:

"Well, look who finally decided to join us."

Maybe try:

"Good to see you in the office, how was your morning?"

Instead of getting fired by saying:

"Do you plan on doing any work today?"

Maybe try:

"Is there something preventing you from getting your work done today?"

Instead of getting fired by saying:

"Your dedication to mediocrity is truly inspiring."

Maybe try:

"Let's review the goals and quality expectations."

Instead of getting fired by saying:

"**Don't strain yourself by putting in any f*cking effort.**"

Maybe try:

"*You seem a bit distracted. Is everything okay?*"

Instead of getting fired by saying:

"It's amazing how you manage to mess up even the simplest tasks."

Maybe try:

"Let's review your workflow together to ensure success."

Instead of getting fired by saying:

"You have an impressive way of doing exactly the bare minimum to get by."

Maybe try:

"I see you have made some progress; what challenges you need help with?"

Instead of getting fired by saying:

> **"Bravo! You've successfully achieved absolutely nothing."**

Maybe try:

> *"Let's discuss how to accomplish our goals effectively."*

Instead of getting fired by saying:

> **"Are you intentionally trying to annoy everyone?"**

Maybe try:

> *"Maybe we can all use a little break and come back with a more cooperative mindset."*

Instead of getting fired by saying:

"Your arrogance is truly insufferable."

Maybe try:

"Let's remember everyone contributes to this project."

Instead of getting fired by saying:

"You are a misogynist, racist bigot."

Maybe try:

"Please don't use that kind of language in the workplace."

Made in United States
Orlando, FL
12 December 2023